Literacy and Language
Pupils' Book

3

Janey Pursglove and **Charlotte Raby**

Series developed by **Ruth Miskin**

OXFORD
UNIVERSITY PRESS

OXFORD
UNIVERSITY PRESS

Great Clarendon Street, Oxford, OX2 6DP,
United Kingdom

Oxford University Press is a department of the
University of Oxford. It furthers the University's
objective of excellence in research, scholarship,
and education by publishing worldwide.
Oxford is a registered trade mark of Oxford University
Press in the UK and in certain other countries

British Library Cataloguing in Publication Data
Data available

ISBN: 978-0-19-833074-5

10 9 8 7 6 5 4

Paper used in the production of this book is a natural,
recyclable product made from wood grown in sustainable
forests. The manufacturing process conforms to the
environmental regulations of the country of origin.

Printed in China by Imago

Acknowledgements

Cover illustration by Anaïs Goldemberg

Illustrations by: Laura Anderson; Mark Chambers; Clare
Elsom; Ben Galbraith; Anaïs Goldemberg; Marcin Piwowarski;
Laura Hughes; Stefano Tambellini; Andrew Painter

The publishers would like to thank the following for
the permission to reproduce photographs: **p8l**: Amanda
Nicholls/Shutterstock; **p8r**: Tischenko Irina/Shutterstock;
p10: Mushakesa/Shutterstock; **p14t**: Leigh Richardson/
Shutterstock; **p14m**: Specta/Shutterstock; **p14b**: South
West Images Scotland/Alamy; **p15**: David Woolfenden/
Shutterstock; **p36-37**: Citi Jo/Shutterstock; **p41**: LongQuattro/
Shutterstock; **p42**: zahradales/Shutterstock; **p53l**: pixelparticle/
Shutterstock; **p53r**: Anton Balazh/Shutterstock; **p54/55**:
mironov/Shutterstock; **p61**: with kind permission from Jamila
Gavin; **p62**: musicman/Shutterstock; **p63**: Theodore Mattas/
Shutterstock; all other images by OUP

TEACHERS:
For inspirational support plus
free resources and eBooks
www.oxfordprimary.co.uk

PARENTS:
Help your child's learning
with essential tips, phonics
support and free eBooks
www.oxfordowl.co.uk

Contents

SAND WIZARDS

Reading

① Word power

Partner 1 read the phrase and its meaning.
Partner 2 read the sentence containing the phrase.

★ **dark, depressing frown** – worried, sad or even moody look with a wrinkled forehead

"I don't understand – I've tried but I still can't do it!" said Harry, with a *dark, depressing frown* on his face.

★ **so relieved** – felt good and relaxed because something unpleasant or worrying stopped or did not happen

When the teacher said, "No test today!" I was *so relieved* that I smiled at her.

★ **with a heart as light as a feather** – feeling happy without any worries

It was the last day of term so I ran home *with a heart as light as a feather*.

② Read a story 3

Discuss the questions.

A Why do you think that Cole has problems making friends?

B Why do you think that Cole ignores the boy at first?

C How do you think Cole felt when he thought Evan was ignoring him in the queue?

D Why do you think that Cole started to smash up his sandcastle?

③ Setting and mood

Remind each other which words in the sentences below tell you about the setting.

A The sky was grey, the holiday was nearly over, and everybody else was having a great time.

B But behind Evan was the huge grey ocean, just waiting to rush in and wreck everything.

C The world suddenly seemed full of hope, and for a moment the sun broke through the clouds, turning the ocean a warm and friendly blue.

Choose some words from the Word bank to describe how Cole was feeling in each of the sentences above.

Word bank

gloomy	anxious	relieved
fed up	excited	dull and bored
worried	troubled	confident

④ What if not...?

Discuss these What if not...? questions.

A What if not *building a sandcastle*? What if the boys *met near a rock pool*?

B What if not *lonely*? What if Cole were *angry*?

C What if not *on his own*? What if Cole were *with a brother or sister*?

⑤ Grammar: inverted commas

Take turns to read Cole's speech bubbles.

> That's a great sandcastle!

> Do you want any help?

★ **Discuss how to write them as direct speech.**

- What goes inside the inverted commas?

- What comes after the closing inverted commas, e.g. *he shouted, he said, he asked?*

★ **Now write the speech bubbles as direct speech in your Personal log.**

Writing

1 Creating mood

Look at these two pictures. Discuss which words you would use from the Word bank to describe each setting.

Word bank

wild   powerful   immense   azure   still

inviting   endless   darkened   awesome

tranquil   playful   joyful   threatening

cold   colourful   busy

② Write a setting 2

Discuss how you can change the mood of your sentence by:

★ thinking about which adjectives create a happy mood and how you can change them, e.g *gentle breeze* to *chilling breeze*

★ making the sea seem more frightening

★ changing what you can hear, e.g. making the shrieks seem fearful or scared.

Use the Word bank to help you.

Word bank

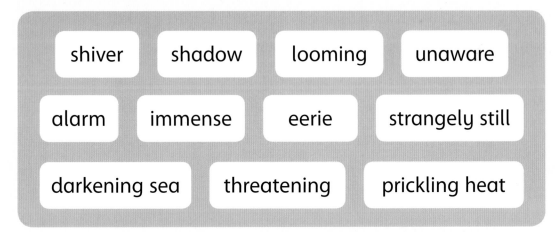

shiver   shadow   looming   unaware

alarm   immense   eerie   strangely still

darkening sea   threatening   prickling heat

Write down your new sentence. Then read it aloud to your partner. Is it threatening? Does the setting seem dangerous?

③ Build a setting 3

Read the paragraphs below and then discuss the questions with your partner.

I had settled by the rocks, and laid out on my towel, resting after splashing and swimming in the cool, refreshing water. I wanted to warm up. As time wore on, I felt the hot sun enveloping me and a gentle breeze whispering on my skin as I drifted into a dream…

Suddenly, from all around, I could hear children's playful squeals of excitement. I had fallen asleep! I leapt up. It was time to join my friends. I scanned the ocean, its colour blending into the bright blue of the sky. I could see the delighted children darting in and out of the glittering azure waves.

"I'm coming in!" I yelled.

I ran to join them. It was a perfect day.

A How would you describe the mood of this setting?

B Are there any words you would change or improve?

④ Write a setting 3

Use the prompts to help you write your description.

Prompts

★ Say what your narrator (the person who is describing the scene) is doing and feeling.

★ Choose the order of your sentences to create a mini story.

★ Use bright, lively words to create an excited, happy mood.

⑤ Write a setting 3 (continued)

Read the paragraphs below and then discuss the questions with your partner.

I had settled out of the shadows of the looming rocks. Laid out on my towel, resting after splashing and swimming in the icy, strangely still water. I needed to warm up. As time wore on, I felt the sticky, hot sun crushing me with its heat. A sudden breeze whipped the hair across my face and I sat up, my eyes fixed on the eerie, endless ocean.

All around, I could hear children's shrill screams of excitement as they ran into the freezing, threatening waves. I scanned the ocean, its colour blending into the grey edge of the sky. I could see the children's legs splattered with foam as they darted into the immense, darkening sea.

At that instant, I saw a shadow lurking just ahead of them. I leapt up.

"Get out of the water!" I yelled.

I ran to save them. It was a terrifying day.

A How would you describe the mood of this setting?

B Are there any words you would change or improve?

Use the prompts to help you write your description.

Prompts

★ Give details about your narrator (who is telling the story) to help set the scene.

★ Make sure your narrator notices the strange shape in the water – that his or her friends can't see.

★ Think about what the narrator might say to warn their friends.

★ Choose the order of your sentences carefully to create tension.

★ Use words to create a threatening, dangerous mood.

(1) Zoom in on information

Take turns to read the sentences below. Decide with your partner whether they give specific information or general information.

A Whitby is a small seaside resort set on a steep hillside.

B Many family campsites have everything you need to make your holiday fun.

C You can usually stay in chalets or caravans.

D The Tate St Ives gallery is in Cornwall.

② Putting information in order

Take turns to read the information about five seaside resorts below.

Discuss the pluses and minuses of each resort. Make notes in your Personal log.

Lulworth Cove: A small fishing village with a beautiful sandy beach, an amazing rock arch, a castle and a car park. There are strong currents so take care when swimming!

Brighton: A bustling city with long pebbly beaches and an amusement pier. Great for shopping and places to eat. Cool surfers, windsurfers and body-boarders hang out among the sunbathers. It can get very busy!

Anglesey: A wild, beautiful island with rugged beaches and lots of space. Many small fishing villages to visit and great for walking and camping.

Stranraer: A great leisure centre in the town and beautiful surrounding countryside. Nearby is Castle Kennedy, as well as Portpatrick, a small fishing village. Along the coast you can swim or snorkel in the clear water and see sea mammals as well as fish.

Whitby: A small resort set on a steep hillside. It has a lively mix of cafes and shops; there is plenty to do! You can hire beach huts to enjoy spending long days on the sandy beaches. It can get very windy and cold in winter.

A Tune of Lies

Reading

① Playscript language

Take turns to read the words below and use them in a sentence.

character	dialogue	stage directions
	setting	scene

② Read a playscript 3

Discuss the questions.

A Who or what is Fib?

B Can Sam and Amy see Fib?

C Why do you think Lucy tells lies?

D Will Amy and Sam trust Lucy in the future? Why/why not?

③ Quiz the character

Take turns to be the Agony Aunt and Lucy.

Here are some questions to help when you are the Agony Aunt.

A When did you first notice Fib in your life?

B What other things did Fib try to get you to say?

C What exactly did you do to try to stop Fib making you say these things?

D How did you feel when you told the lies?

E Why did you think you needed to tell the fibs?

F How would you like me to help?

After the role play, discuss what advice you would offer Lucy.

④ Not just...

Take turns to think of powerful words to finish the sentences. Use the Word bank to help you.

A Lucy said she was *not just* a good harp player, she was…

B After Lucy told lies she was *not just* upset, she was…

C The lies were *not just* awful, they were…

Word bank

amazing	horrific	dreadful	fantastic
sick with worry	brilliant	terrible tangles	
deeply dismayed	hot and bothered	anxious	

⑤ Explore stage directions
TTYP

Take turns to read the questions.

Discuss what you have learnt about the characters from the stage directions.

A Do you think Lucy is in control of what is happening to her? Find a stage direction to show why you think this.

B How does Fib try to control Lucy? Find a stage direction that shows this.

C What do you think Sam and Amy's immediate reactions will be to what has happened? Discuss what you could write as a stage direction to show this.

(1) What if not…? TTYP

Discuss these What if not…? questions.

A What if not *Fib crushed*? What if *Lucy had been crushed*?

B What if not *new*? What if Lucy had *always lived* in the area?

C What if not *kind*? What if Sam and Amy were *unkind* to Lucy?

② Step into the script

Partner 1 read the new *A Tune of Lies* scene, below. Then re-read it with Partner 2 improvising Lucy's missing speech.

Fib   You think you are so clever telling Amy and Sam that it's all a lie! Do you think they are going to like you now? Boring! Boring!

Lucy   (Partner 2 – improvise a response)

Fib   You can't just stop telling lies, you know... I'll pop up whenever I get a chance. No one knows you here really, it'll be so easy to take control!

Lucy   (Partner 2 – improvise a response)

Fib   Oh yes... I forgot you are so interesting...you're a brilliant netball player...an award-winning artist...a fabulous swimmer...you're so talented! Lucy, without ME you are nothing, just another little girl.

Lucy   (Partner 2 – improvise a response)

Fib   Hah! With my lies you are fascinating and people will want to play with me. Stick with me, Lucy, and we'll be fine!

Lucy   (Partner 2 – improvise a response)

③ Write a script 2

Use the prompts below to act out the fight between Fib and Lucy.

⭐ Think how Fib can make Lucy feel unsure of herself and her friendship.

⭐ Think how Fib can taunt Lucy and try to make her lie again. Remind Lucy that without Fib she is boring and not cool at all.

⭐ Lucy needs to stand up to Fib. Can she think of reasons to be strong? Can she believe in her friends?

⭐ Help Lucy win by making her see she is strong. Or help Fib win by making Lucy believe she needs Fib to seem cool and interesting.

4 Write a script 3

Read the prompts below, and think about what is going to happen in your developed version of the script. Then tell your partner about your plan.

Think about how you want to develop Sam's and Amy's character. How do they react as they hear Lucy talk – do they want to help her, or are they frustrated, angry or frightened?

Who decides they should go in – Sam or Amy?
What argument do they use to persuade the other?

Think carefully about the stage direction that describes how Sam and Amy enter the room, e.g. *creeping in, bursting in*?

Who wins the argument in your version – Lucy or Fib? Why?

How do Lucy and Fib react when Sam and Amy walk in?

How will you end your scene?

Now write your scene. Use the notes and dialogue you have drafted in your Personal log to help you.

① Write 1

Remember these Top Tips when you write your instructions.

Make sure your instructions are clear. Have you used the best verb to describe each action?

Make sure your layout is easy to follow. Do you need to use bullet points, numbers, text boxes, diagrams or pictures?

Make sure each section of the instructions is clearly headed, explaining what that part of the writing is about.

Check the Key features checklist. Have you included all the important features?

Key features checklist

✓ Title   ✓ Additional information

✓ Introduction   ✓ Imperative verbs

✓ List of materials   ✓ Adverbs of time and manner

✓ Subheadings   ✓ Pictures with captions

② Evaluate and edit

Read the evaluation points below with your partner.

My instructions for making a bottle band:

★ lay out information clearly, e.g. *with subheadings, pictures*

★ use precise language so the reader knows exactly what to do.

Grammar:

★ includes imperative verbs, to make it clear that I am instructing the reader to do something

★ includes adverbs of time, so the reader knows which order to do things in, e.g. *First, Then*.

Discuss how well Partner 1's writing has included the points. Then do the same for Partner 2's writing.

A Tale of Two Robots

Reading

① Read a story 3

Discuss the questions.

A Why do you think that Callum won't tidy his own bedroom?

B Did Robert the robot behave as you thought he would?

C Why do you think Robert wanted to go to school with Callum?

D How do you think Callum felt when he found out that Shannon was an inventor too?

(2) Word power

Partner 1 read the word and its meaning.
Partner 2 read the sentence containing the word.

★ **absent-mindedly** – dreamily

I *absent-mindedly* put on my trousers back to front!

★ **tentatively** – cautiously, uncertainly

The dog sniffed the new food *tentatively*.

★ **fumed** – raged

"Who pinched my chocolate?" *fumed* the boy.

★ **brusquely** – roughly, abruptly

"Stop messing about!" he said *brusquely*.

(3) Grammar: determiners *a* and *an*

Decide whether the robots should use *a* or *an*.

Robert: Guess what? There was **a/an** apple core stuffed in Callum's shoes!

Nita: Shannon left **a/an** sticky sweet under her pillow. Disgusting!

Robert: Well, I've just bought **a/an** incredible cleaning spray.

Nita: I could do with **a/an** bottle of that myself!

④ Most powerful?

Read this part of *A Tale of Two Robots* together.

At break time, everyone crowded round Robert. They didn't talk to him, but kept asking Callum questions.

"Why has he got a coat hanger sticking out of his neck?"

"Because that's all I had to make his shoulders with," replied Callum **brusquely**.

"Can he exterminate people?"

"Of course he can't! He's only a room-cleaning robot," Callum snapped.

"He's well weird."

At that moment, Callum glanced up at Robert's face. He could've sworn that the robot's metallic features were somehow creased into an expression of sadness, almost bordering on tears.

"Why don't you leave him alone?" a girl's voice piped up. It was Shannon, one of Callum's classmates.

Everyone began drifting away, leaving Shannon alone with Callum and Robert. She took Callum to one side. "I think Robert's lonely," she whispered.

Who do you think is the most powerful character in this part of the story?

Is it:

A Callum?

B The other children asking all the questions?

C Robert?

D Shannon?

Remember to explain why.

What do you think is the most important moment of the whole story?

Is it:

1 When Mum threatens to clean the bedroom herself?

2 When Callum decides he needs a room-cleaning robot?

3 When the robot comes alive?

4 When Robert is introduced to Nita the robot?

Remember to explain why.

Writing

① **What if not...?**

Discuss these What if not...? questions.

A What if not a *success*? What if Callum's robot invention had *gone wrong*?

B What if not *pleased* to have Robert in her classroom? What if Ms Shelley were *angry* that Callum brought his robot to school?

C What if not *happy*? What if Robert and Nita were *fed up* with cleaning bedrooms all day, every day?

② Dramatic reconstruction 1

Partner 1 you are Nita. Tell your partner about the trip to the zoo, from your point of view.

Use these prompts to plan and practise what you are going to say.

★ You tried to stop Robert from going in the chimps' enclosure.

★ You were embarrassed when the zoo keeper yelled at Robert.

★ You were cross that you both had to leave the zoo without seeing any animals.

★ What else might you have felt?

Partner 2 you are Robert. Tell your partner about the trip to the zoo, from your point of view.

Use these prompts to plan and practise what you are going to say.

★ You were disgusted at the state of the chimps' enclosure.

★ You thought you were being helpful by trying to clean it up.

★ You were surprised that the zoo keeper threw you out.

★ What else might you have felt?

① Discussion words

Partner 1 read the word.
Partner 2 read the meaning.

Word	Meaning
statement	a sentence that is not a question or telling you to do something
balanced	giving both sides of an argument
point of view	what someone thinks about a topic
conclusion	the ending, what you decide after you have heard different points of view

Partner 1 read passage A on page 33 to your partner.
Partner 2 read passage B on page 33 to your partner.

Discuss which passage is a balanced discussion and which one only gives one point of view. Remember to explain why.

A Pocket money for children is not a right; it should be a payment for doing chores.

Parents and carers have to shop, cook, clean and wash clothes for children and they don't get paid for doing all that! Why should they give money to children without getting some help? Just because children do schoolwork and other activities, it doesn't mean they haven't got time to help at home as well.

B Some people think that pocket money for children should be payment for doing chores. However, others think that a child should not have to work for their pocket money.

It could be said that parents and carers have to shop, cook, clean and wash clothes for children. They don't get paid for doing all that, so why should they give money to children for doing chores?

On the other hand, some children spend hours doing schoolwork and activities and might not have time to help at home as well.

② Deconstruction 3

Look at these leaflets about dogs and cats.
Take turns to read one section at a time of leaflet A.

A Doggy details!

Dogs can make lovely pets but they need a lot of looking after! Read our information carefully before you rush out and buy a puppy or a dog.

🐾 Dogs greet you like an old friend when you walk through the door. However, dogs do get lonely so you can't leave them alone all day.

🐾 All dogs, big and small, need walking, and exercise is good for humans too. Not so much fun in the wind and rain, though...

🐾 Dogs leave their mess anywhere! Dog owners must clear it up. You can be fined for leaving it in a public place.

🐾 Dogs can be dangerous if they are not trained properly. Sharp teeth can cause nasty bites to humans.

🐾 Barking is one way that dogs communicate. Loud barking can be annoying to neighbours, though.

Remember! You have to arrange for your dog to be cared for when you go away on holiday. It can be expensive to send it to a pet hotel.

Add some reasons for and against having a pet dog to your mind map.

Now take turns to read one section at a time of leaflet B.

Cat facts...

- Cats can be very relaxing. Stroking a cat can calm you down when you are upset.

- Cats can be a bit boring! They often sleep between 12 - 18 hours a day!

- It is very rare for cats to cause serious injuries to humans – they can scratch your best furniture, though, as they need to keep their claws sharp...

- Cats are hard to keep safe. Road traffic accidents are the biggest cause of injuries to cats.

- Cats are playful and love toys that they can chase. They know their own minds, though, and will only play or be cuddled when *they* want to!

- Cats can kill birds and small mammals. This can be upsetting to see but it is natural behaviour for cats.

Add some reasons for and against having a pet cat to your mind map.

Poetic language

① Read a poem 1

Read this riddle out loud together then discuss the questions.

I thunder,
I creep,
I spit,
I seep.
I trickle,
I gush.
I'm slow,
I rush.
I'm in a cloud,
I'm in the sea.
I'm trapped!
I'm free...

A What do you think it is?

B How did you work it out?

- Which words were the most helpful? Which words were the least helpful?

- Why do you think it says 'I'm trapped'? How or where could it be trapped?

② Read a poem 2

Read this riddle out loud together then discuss the questions.

Stone rattler
Dam battler
Bubble foamer
Land roamer
Song gurgler
Life burglar
Raft thriller
Sea filler.

A Which line makes the most powerful picture in your mind? Describe the picture to your partner.

B Is the rhythm fast or slow? Is it the same beat all the way through?

With your partner, think of two more words to add to the poem.

③ **Special phrases**

Partner 1 read each phrase with lots of expression!
Partner 2 read its meaning.
Both partners read about its imagery.

> **Vocabulary check**
> **imagery**   pictures created from words

Special phrase	Meaning	Imagery
'Cold cloud spit her out'	Water in a cloud falls as rain.	The cloud wants to get rid of the heavy water so it spits it out.
'Mountains weep and dream'	Rain falls on the mountain, making streams.	The streams falling down the mountainsides make the mountains look as if they are crying or weeping.
'A man-made hand stops her dead With a dam'	A dam is made by humans and it can stop natural water running its course.	The dam is like a giant hand that is so big and strong, it will not let the powerful water get past it.

Which is your favourite Special phrase? Why?

④ Poetic features 2

Vocabulary check

alliteration	words close to each other with the same first letter sound
rhyme	a similar sound in the ending of words
repetition	repeated words or phrases

Read the lines (A, B and C) from the poem 'Water-cycle' then match up the correct think bubbles (1, 2 and 3).

A 'Tap, kettle, cup of tea, into me and out of me'

1 I like the way rhyming words are in the same line, and give a feeling of waking up in the morning, full of energy and excitement.

B 'Wide awake, thrills like a milkshake shivers'

2 I like the repetition which makes me think of something falling deep inside the earth, and echoing as it drops.

C 'Down, down, down underground, rushing round'

3 The alliteration of words at the beginning reminds me of cups and saucers clinking together.

Writing

1 Personal log: strange combinations

TTYP

Vocabulary check

compound word   two words joined together to make a new word with its own meaning

These compound words have got mixed up and now they are nonsense compound words!

toothfish	spacesnake	rattledancer
tapcorn	goldpaste	popship

TTYP to discuss what strange pictures they make in your mind!

Sort them out with your partner to make real compound words.

When you are sure they are right, write them in your Personal log.

② Write a poem 1

Here are two compound words:

★ firework ★ waterfall

Partner 1 describe the picture in your mind when you read 'firework'.

Partner 2 describe the picture in your mind when you read 'waterfall'.

Now think of some more phrases to describe a firework. Use the word boxes below to help you.

Onomatopoeic words	More fireworks words
whizz fizz bang pop crackle shoot whoosh hiss poof zoom whistle sizzle vroom	explode burn fire fiery hot flame bright shower blaze shine glow twinkle sparkle

Endings to try:

_____ing (whizzing)

_____s (pops)

_____es (whooshes)

_____er (banger)

_____ y (fizzy)

Say your new phrase out loud to your partner before you write it in your Personal log. (Then turn the page.)

Think of some more phrases to describe a waterfall.
Use the word boxes below to help you.

Onomatopoeic words:

splash rush gurgle
bubble boom
rumble rattle gush
roar crash swoosh
whoosh

More waterfall words:

cold foam shower
cascade sparkle
flow pour spill
tumble flood

Endings to try:

_____ing (rushing)

_____s (roars)

_____es (crashes)

_____er (boomer)

_____ y (bubbly)

They are gurgling sparklers!

Say your new phrase out loud to your partner before
you write it in your Personal log.

③ Evaluate

Read the poem out loud with your partner.
Use the prompts to discuss the poem.

Angry bones are
raging rattlers.
Angry bones are
cross clatterers.
They are such anger clangers!

Water cycles are
wave wheelers.
Water cycles are
pedal sloppers.
They are such water swooshers!

Prompts

A Choose the phrase that
describes angry bones
best of all:
raging rattlers
cross clatterers
anger clangers

B Do you think this is a
nonsense poem? Why?

C Which is your favourite
onomatopoeic word?
Why?

D Tap out the beat of the
poem as you read it.

1 Pictures into words

A Look at this life cycle diagram with your partner.

Partner 1 explain what this diagram is showing.
Partner 2 say whether you agree with the explanation.

Life cycle diagram

B Now look at the chain diagram on the next page.

Partner 1 explain what this diagram is showing.
Partner 2 say whether you agree with the explanation.

Chain diagram

Grammar: prefixes

Take turns to read the words.

| microphone | supermarket | automatic | prehistoric |

Discuss which part of each word is the prefix.
Write the prefixes in your Personal log.

Then read the words below and discuss which prefix
is being described.

A before **B** tiny **C** bigger than is usual **D** on its own

Smash and Grab!

Reading

① Word power 1

Take turns to read the phrases below. Tell your partner what pictures they make you see in your mind.

> encircled by its high stone wall

> congestion and bustle

> magnificent marble staircase

> The children, perplexed, hurried after Mrs McCreevy

> ran breathlessly

② Read a story 3

Discuss the questions.

A When do you think Katie and Adil first realised that something was wrong?

B How did the bees' behaviour help the children to solve the crime?

C What clues in the story helped you work out who the robber was?

D Who did you think was the best detective: Adil, Katie or Sergeant Pemberton?

③ Grammar: adverbs and word families

Adverbs

Partner 1 read the adverb and root word.
Partner 2 read what the adverb means.
Together, make up a sentence using the adverb.

A The adverb is *gently*. The root word is *gentle*.
Gentle means calm, kind and quiet.

B The adverb is *curiously*. The root word is *curious*.
Curious means wanting to find out about things.

C The adverb is *breathlessly*. The root word is *breath*.
Breath is the air that you take into your lungs and send
out again.

D The adverb is *loudly*. The root word is *loud*.
Loud means noisy.

Word families

**Take turns to read the rows of words that belong to
the same family.**

More Word Families		
energy	energetic	energetically
hide	hiding	hid
speed	speeding	sped
sting	stinging	stung

4 Personal log

With your partner, read the sentence below and find the adverb. Remember that an adverb gives more detail about a verb.

"Well, you can see I'm not hiding those!" snapped the red-faced man, crossing his arms angrily.

Think up a new sentence using the adverb and write it in your Personal log.

5 What if not...?

Discuss these What if not...? questions.

★ What if not *a beehive*? What if the thief had hidden the jewels *somewhere else* in the castle grounds?

★ What if not *a greatcoat, flying hat, goggles and gas mask*? What if the thief had taken *something else* from the museum to use for protection, like a suit of armour?

★ What if not *jewels*? What if the thief had stolen *a valuable painting, or a special book*?

★ What if not *the pretty woman*? What if *the cross man,* or even *Mrs McCreevy* had stolen the jewels?

Writing

① What next?

Take turns to read each sentence with expression.

The children, mystified, leaned closer to Mr Masters as he peered anxiously through the open door. As they edged into the bright nursery, Mr Masters let out a sigh of dismay at the sight of all the toys and furniture covering the floor. All of Queen Victoria's royal baby clothes had vanished!

Now write your own version of this paragraph in your Personal log. Remember to think about:

★ how the children feel

★ how Mr Masters looks into the room

★ how they enter the room

★ how Mr Masters reacts to what he sees

★ what has happened to Queen Victoria's royal baby clothes.

Take turns to read what happens next.

"This is awful!" groaned Mr Masters. He got out his mobile phone, punched in a number and started to talk quietly. Almost immediately an alarm sounded and the children could hear doors shutting throughout the building.

"I've shut down the building," explained Mr Masters. "No one can get out now. I just hope I was quick enough. Those clothes are irreplaceable."

"Don't worry," soothed Mrs McCreevy. "These wonderful children helped me before and I'm sure they can help you too. Actually, I think Sergeant Pemberton should be here by now. Shall I call him?"

At that very moment, the gruff voice of Sergeant Pemberton could be heard coming up the stairs. "I caught these three trying to flee the building. Perhaps we should start by asking them some questions."

② Write a story 1

Use the picture prompt to help you decide what is stolen and where it is hidden in your mystery story.

Then discuss the questions below with your partner.

A Where did the crime take place?

B What was taken?

C Who are the suspects?

D What clues are there to help work out where the stolen item has been hidden and who the thief is?

③ Write a story 3

Use these Top Tips for writing a mystery story.

★ Don't give away all the mystery before the end. You can reveal what has happened but not who has done it!

★ Leave clues for the reader so they can solve the mystery alongside the characters.

★ Keep the mystery moving – don't have all the action happening in one place.

★ Use dialogue to move the story on.

★ Show characters' feelings by describing their reactions to new situations.

(1) Word power

Partner 1 read the word and its meaning.
Partner 2 read the sentence containing the word.

★ **imitation** – a copy of something
The *imitation* handbag fell apart in the rain.

★ **simulated** – not real, pretend or fake
The *simulated* flight made me feel really ill, even though we never left the ground!

★ **habitable** – somewhere fit to live in
The shelter was dry and *habitable* so we decided to stay there.

★ **atmosphere** – the air around the Earth
The Earth's *atmosphere* is made up of many different gases.

★ **microbes** – living microscopic things such as bacteria and viruses
When you sneeze thousands of *microbes* fly into the air. Yuck!

53

② **Key features of non-chronological reports**

Take turns to read each key feature and then find an example of it in the Anthology (pages 63–67).

Key features

title   subheadings

facts (including dates and numbers)

present tense   technical language

bullet points   diagrams   labels

photographs   captions   text boxes

proper nouns (names given to one particular place or thing)

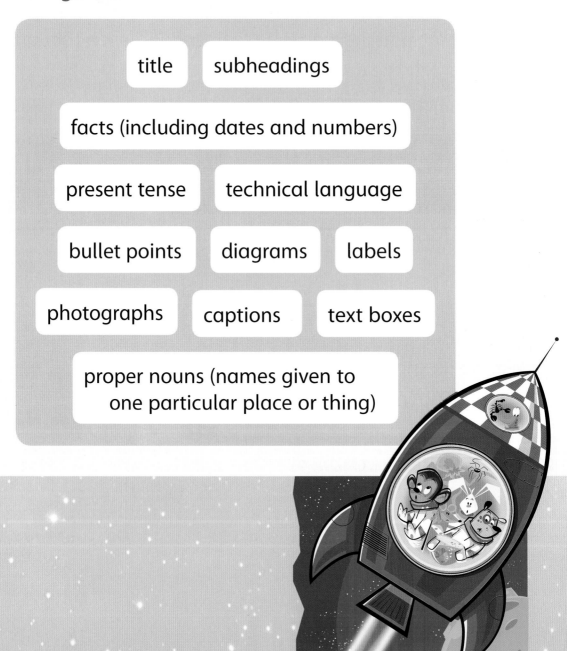

③ Personal log

Use these Top Tips to help you write your notes.

★ Before you write the notes make sure you know what you are looking for and listen or look out for that information.

★ Make a short heading for a group of notes about the same subject.

★ Only write the key words/phrases.

★ Some words can be abbreviated to make it quicker to take notes, e.g. *Space Curiosity* could become *SC*.

★ Write facts you want to use, such as names, dates and places but not extras – you can always check back for more information later.

④ Make a broadcast

Take turns to read through the Top Tips for a good broadcast.

★ Make sure you speak clearly and slowly.

★ Get the main facts across using simple language.

★ Explain any technical words so the audience understands them. (Use the glossary to help you.)

The Enchantress of the Sands

Reading

① Word power

Partner 1 read the word and its meaning.
Partner 2 read the sentence containing the word.

★ **enchantress** – woman who can make spells or enchant

The *enchantress* began to sing as she stirred the magic potion.

★ **herdsman** – man who looks after cattle, sheep or other herds of animals.

The *herdsman* chased the sly fox away from his sheep.

★ **begone** – go away

The king scowled at the foolish knight. "*Begone!* Out of my sight!" he thundered.

★ **rejoiced** – celebrated, full of joy

The whole family *rejoiced* when they heard I had won the competition.

② Personal log

Choose a setting from below.

| the tree house | the desert | the enchantress's hut |

Write a sentence to describe the setting in your Personal log.

– § –

Partner 1 read your sentence to your partner.

Partner 2 close your eyes and listen. Tell your partner what picture you can see in your mind.

Together, use the prompts below to improve the sentence. Then swap over.

Prompts

A Have you described what you can see?

B Have you described how hot or cool the setting is?

C Have you made your setting seem safe or full of danger?

D Have you described the sounds that you could hear if you stood in the setting?

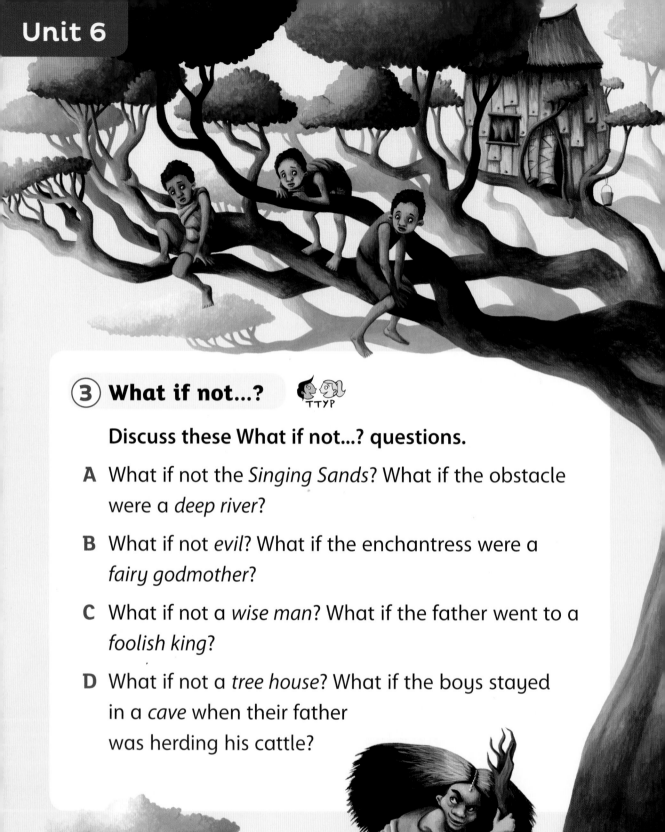

③ What if not...?

TTYP

Discuss these What if not...? questions.

A What if not the *Singing Sands*? What if the obstacle were a *deep river*?

B What if not *evil*? What if the enchantress were a *fairy godmother*?

C What if not a *wise man*? What if the father went to a *foolish king*?

D What if not a *tree house*? What if the boys stayed in a *cave* when their father was herding his cattle?

(1) Story phrases

Take turns to retell *The Enchantress of the Sands*, using the story map in your Personal log to help you.

Try to use some of these Story phrases:

On the far side

It was because

Every day,

So every day, when

And every evening,

But one day

But because

The next evening

The next day

When the herdsman

When he got to

On the other side

For a moment

…but before she…

② Write a story 2

Use the prompts to help write the climax of your story.

Prompts

★ Make sure you create a tense, exciting atmosphere. The enchantress's hut should seem a scary place.

★ Use dialogue to create tension. Remember that the characters don't always say what they are thinking!

★ Show what the characters are thinking by the way they move or how you describe them, e.g. *with a cunning smile/with a sly grin.*

★ Choose your verbs carefully, to bring the action to life.

1 Comparing biography and autobiography

Take turns to read the phrases below. Decide whether each phrase is from the biography or the autobiography.

But me, I boasted

I lived in a palace

Her father and mother were both teachers

she looked very different to the other children

she would weave stories about the palace

especially on the occasions that we came over to England

② Taking notes 3

Read the Fact File below. Discuss the information it gives. Make notes on your Research questions note-taker.

Fact File 2

Name, Date and place of birth:
Jean Yaya, 24th August 1982,
Abidjan, Ivory Coast

Details of journey to the UK: I saved up my money and I flew to Gatwick Airport. It took many hours to fly but I loved it. I haven't been in an aeroplane since. At Gatwick there was a long queue at passport control so it took some time to get through. The man called me and asked where was I going to stay. I explained I was visiting my sister. He stamped my passport and I could go through.

Why you came to the UK: My father is from the UK, although he lives with my mother in Abidjan now. My sister came to the UK to study. She is very clever and has done well for herself. She suggested that I should come and study. She said there is work if you are willing to work hard. I am glad my sister is here or I would be very lonely.

What you miss about home: I miss my family and celebrating our holidays most of all.

Life in the UK: I live in Manchester with my sister and her family. I work driving deliveries and I am at college. I am studying engineering at college.

③ Grammar: paragraphs

Take turns to read these sentences.

A The feathers can also be used for camouflage or to attract a male or female.

B They have dry scaly skin that is waterproof.

C Zoos can help people learn about the importance of protecting animals that are endangered in the wild, such as tigers.

D Ostriches are the largest birds in the world.

E Elephants are the only mammals that cannot jump.

F They move by creeping or crawling along the ground and some reptiles can move very quickly.

G All mammals are warm blooded and have some hair on their bodies.

With your partner, decide which paragraphs the sentences could be added to in the Zoos text.

④ Write 2

Check whether you have used the Key features below in your biography.

Key features

★ Third person pronouns (*he*, *she*, *they* or a name)

★ The past tense (verbs often have -ed endings)

★ Names of places

★ Information such as facts, dates and figures

★ A bit of personal information

★ Chronology (events told in the order they happened)

★ Adverbs of time to show the order of events